InterActions
small group series

Reclaiming
Six
Endangered
Qualities

CHARACTER

Interactions Small Group Series

Authenticity: Being Honest with God and Others
Character: Reclaiming Six Endangered Qualities
Commitment: Developing Deeper Devotion to Christ
Community: Building Relationships within God's Family
Essential Christianity: Practical Steps for Spiritual Growth
Fruit of the Spirit: Living the Supernatural Life
Getting a Grip: Finding Balance in Your Daily Life
Jesus: Seeing Him More Clearly
Lessons on Love: Building Deeper Relationships
Living in God's Power: Finding God's Strength for Life's Challenges
Love in Action: Experiencing the Joy of Serving
Marriage: Building Real Intimacy
Meeting God: Psalms for the Highs and Lows of Life
New Identity: Discovering Who You Are in Christ
Parenting: How to Raise Spiritually Healthy Kids
Prayer: Opening Your Heart to God
Reaching Out: Sharing God's Love Naturally
The Real Deal: Discover the Rewards of Authentic Relationships
Significance: Understanding God's Purpose for Your Life
Transformation: Letting God Change You from the Inside Out

InterActions
small group series

Reclaiming
Six
Endangered
Qualities

CHARACTER

BILL HYBELS

WITH KEVIN AND SHERRY HARNEY

ZONDERVAN™

GRAND RAPIDS, MICHIGAN 49530 USA

WILLOW
Willow Creek Resources

We want to hear from you. Please send your comments about this book to us in care of zreview@zondervan.com. Thank you.

ZONDERVAN™

Character
Copyright © 1997 by Willow Creek Association

Requests for information should be addressed to:

Zondervan, *Grand Rapids, Michigan 49530*

ISBN-10: 0-310-26602-5
ISBN-13: 978-0-310-26602-0

Interior design by Rick Devon & Michelle Espinoza

Printed in the United States of America

07 08 09 10 11 12 /❖ DCI/ 10 9 8 7 6 5

CONTENTS

INTERACTIONS

In 1992, Willow Creek Community Church, in partnership with Zondervan and the Willow Creek Association, released a curriculum for small groups entitled the Walking with God series. In just three years, almost a half million copies of these small group study guides were being used in churches around the world. The phenomenal response to this curriculum affirmed the need for relevant and biblical small group materials.

At the writing of this curriculum, there are nearly 3,000 small groups meeting regularly within the structure of Willow Creek Community Church. We believe this number will increase as we continue to place a central value on small groups. Many other churches throughout the world are growing in their commitment to small group ministries as well, so the need for resources is increasing.

In response to this great need, the Interactions small group series has been developed. Willow Creek Association and Zondervan have joined together to create a whole new approach to small group materials. These discussion guides are meant to challenge group members to a deeper level of sharing, to create lines of accountability, to move followers of Christ into action, and to help group members become fully devoted followers of Christ.

SUGGESTIONS FOR INDIVIDUAL STUDY

1. Begin each session with prayer. Ask God to help you understand the passage and to apply it to your life.
2. A good modern translation, such as the New International Version, the New American Standard Bible, or the New Revised Standard Version, will give you the most help. Questions in this guide are based on the New International Version.
3. Read and reread the passage(s). You must know what the passage says before you can understand what it means and how it applies to you.
4. Write your answers in the spaces provided in the study guide. This will help you to express clearly your understanding of the passage.
5. Keep a Bible dictionary handy. Use it to look up unfamiliar words, names, or places.

SUGGESTIONS FOR GROUP STUDY

1. Come to the session prepared. Careful preparation will greatly enrich your time in group discussion.
2. Be willing to join in the discussion. The leader of the group will not be lecturing, but will encourage people to discuss what they have learned in the passage. Plan to share what God has taught you in your individual study.
3. Stick to the passage being studied. Base your answers on the verses being discussed rather than on outside authorities such as commentaries or your favorite author or speaker.
4. Try to be sensitive to the other members of the group. Listen attentively when they speak, and be affirming whenever you can. This will encourage more hesitant members of the group to participate.
5. Be careful not to dominate the discussion. By all means participate, but allow others to have equal time.
6. If you are the discussion leader, you will find additional suggestions and helpful ideas in the Leader's Notes.

ADDITIONAL RESOURCES AND TEACHING MATERIALS

At the end of this study guide you will find a collection of resources and teaching materials to help you in your growth as a follower of Christ. You will also find resources that will help your church develop and build fully devoted followers of Christ.

Introduction:
Reclaiming Six
Endangered Qualities

As I have been studying the topic of character, a strange idea came to mind. Imagine the state of Illinois, where I live, doing a variation on their state lottery. Instead of winning money, one person would win a fully developed character trait. In other words, no multimillion-dollar jackpot for the lucky winner, but one character trait that person really wanted.

Every day millions of people spend lots of money in the hope of winning a big jackpot. I wonder how many people would toss their dollar into the pot if the payoff was a fully developed character trait. Could you see people standing in long lines in the hope of winning courage? Or millions of people risking a buck or two on the long shot that they might win discipline, confidence, or patience? How many people would play if the grand prize was endurance or contentment?

This might seem like a strange concept, but think about it for a minute. Which is worth more in life—ten million dollars or contentment? Which is more valuable, one hundred thousand dollars a year for the rest of your life or self-discipline? Before you answer too quickly, really think about it. I believe each of the character traits in this series of interactions is worth more than any lottery jackpot.

Sadly, each of the character traits I've noted are endangered. As a matter of fact, some of them are close to being put on the extinct list. None can be purchased or won in a lottery; they must be developed over time. None comes easily, but all are valuable beyond compare. My invitation is for you to search your heart and see where you need to develop each of these characteristics. What would your life be like if you had courage, self-discipline, confidence, patience, contentment, and endurance? My prayer is that God will grow each of these character qualities in your life.

Bill Hybels

COURAGE

THE BIG PICTURE

My dad fought in World War II, so I grew up listening to war stories. His stories about human courage in the face of fear and struggle had a magnetic effect on me—I could not pull away from his side when he told them.

My father was sort of an eccentric person. He once bought a sailboat in Ireland and sailed it across the Atlantic Ocean, enduring a five-day hurricane and facing many other challenges on the open sea. Before he set sail he collected and read a small library of books on sailing, so he had some idea what he was in for. But it was still a trip to be remembered for a lifetime.

Over the years I think I have read every book my dad collected in anticipation of that journey. He had books about ocean crossings, shipping disasters, the sinking of the Titanic, and all sorts of other ocean adventures. Whenever I would get to the part where the ship was going down and there weren't enough life jackets, my heart would start to race and my throat would get dry. When some guy said bravely, "Take my life jacket," committing himself to the cold, shark-infested waters of the ocean, something happened inside of me. Every time I read an account of someone saying, "Take my seat in the life boat. I'll go down," my breath would get short and my pulse would start to race. This was real-life courage!

The truth is, anytime I hear about someone demonstrating courage rather than cowardliness, something happens inside of me. I find myself saying, "That's what I want to be like. I wish I had more of that in my life. I don't want my life debilitated by fear. I don't want to live life paralyzed by worry. I don't want to compromise my convictions. I don't want to quit when I face difficult challenges. I don't want to be a coward. I want to be a person of courage!"

1 Describe an act of courage you have witnessed.

What are some of the ordinary, day-to-day acts of courage that people perform without ever being noticed?

A BIBLICAL PORTRAIT

Read 2 Timothy 1:7–12

2 The apostle Paul exhibits a spirit of courage and deep commitment in this passage. What seems to drive or motivate him to remain courageous?

How does the example of Paul challenge or move you to want to be more courageous?

3 This passage says God does not put a spirit of "timidity" or cowardice in His followers. Illustrate what you think a spirit of timidity looks like in *one* of these areas:

- In a marriage
- In a friendship
- In the marketplace
- In raising children

SHARPENING THE FOCUS

Read Snapshot "Spiritual Courage"

SPIRITUAL COURAGE

I want to dissect the concept of courage into smaller pieces so we can really get a look at it. We need to examine how courage relates to different dimensions of our lives. First, I want to focus on spiritual courage. You see, we don't often think of courage in spiritual terms. But we have all heard the well-worn expression, "Christianity is for weak people." Some people think Christianity is for cowards and crutch-users.

I've always been fascinated by this accusation because I have found the exact opposite to be true. I marvel at the incredible amount of courage it takes to even *become* a Christian. Following Christ demands the best we have. It calls for more than we can give. Living as a fully devoted follower of Christ takes courage on a daily basis for the rest of our lives!

4 Respond to this statement: Christianity is for cowards; it is a crutch for the weak!

How did you exercise courage when you first became a follower of Christ?

5 How does living as a fully devoted follower of Christ demand courage from you in *one* of the following areas:

- In your workplace
- Where you live
- In your friendships with seekers
- In your family

Read Snapshot "Moral Courage"

MORAL COURAGE

Have you ever thought about how much moral courage it takes to operate ethically and honestly in the marketplace? Too often we lack the courage to admit the truth. We want to please customers so we say, "The shipment will be there Monday," even though we know it won't be there until Wednesday.

Christians are also called to be courageous morally when it comes to financial matters. Each year, as we pay income tax, we see who is courageous and who is a coward. We either demonstrate moral courage by reporting all our income, or we cave in and have to admit to being moral cowards.

And how about staying sexually pure in a sex-crazed culture? It seems to me that it takes a tremendous amount of courage to stand by your convictions even when everyone else says you are hopelessly idealistic, old-fashioned, and a little bit strange.

---

6 What does moral courage look like in *one* of these areas:

- When it comes time to do your taxes
- When sexual temptation lurks at the door
- When you have given into a temptation and been caught
- When you are tempted to bend the truth to avoid conflict

7

How and where in your life are you being pressured to cave in morally and not exercise courage? Explain.

What support can your small group members offer you to help you live with courage in this area of your life?

Read Snapshot "Relational Courage"

RELATIONAL COURAGE

When people ask me, "What does it take to build a meaningful marriage?" I am sure to say, "A good marriage is made up of varying ingredients, but one thing I know for sure is that it takes courage." For a relationship to flourish in a marriage, there must be intimacy. And it takes an enormous amount of courage to become vulnerable and self-disclosing. A coward can't say, "This is who I am. I'm not proud of it, but this is who I am."

This same depth of courage is mandatory for authentic relationships between friends, between parents and children, or between colleagues at work. Courage is always an essential element in an authentic relationship.

8

How have you seen courage build a healthy relationship?

Describe a time you saw cowardice undermine and destroy a relationship.

9 What is one relationship you need to strengthen by exercising more courage?

What is one thing you will do to courageously strengthen this relationship?

PUTTING YOURSELF IN THE PICTURE

FACING YOUR FEARS

Growing in courage has something to do with facing crippling fears. We tend to think that courageous people were born without fear. In actuality, courageous people are ordinary people like you and me who began, at some point, to face their fears rather than retreat from them. Courageous people have learned that facing fear usually diffuses it, while running from fear tends to intensify it.

My dad knew this principle, and he often challenged me to face my fears. I remember being out on his sailboat on a day when there were huge waves on Lake Michigan. We were coming in between two cement piers and the waves were tossing us one way and the other when my dad said, "I've got to go down below. You take over the helm, Billy."

I knew exactly what my dad was doing. He was waiting until I was terrified out of my mind, and then letting me face my fears. One minute the boat would be heading right toward the cement barrier. I'd crank the wheel over, and then the wave would pitch the boat over to the other side.

Eventually I managed to get safely past the piers. I can still remember being so frightened that I was physically shaking, at which point my dad came back up from below deck and said, "Now, that wasn't so bad, was it?" And sure enough, the next time it was a bit easier. I'm not recommending everyone put their kid at the helm of a boat in rough waters, but you can see the principle at work, can't you? Often facing our fears is the only way to overcome them and develop courage in a specific area of life.

Take time in the coming week to identify one specific area in which you are dealing with fear. What can you do to intentionally face this fear straight on and begin to overcome it and develop courage in your life? You may want to have a member of your small group or a close Christian friend pray for you and walk with you through this courage-building adventure.

SCRIPTURE MEMORY

Take time in the coming week to memorize this passage and reflect deeply on its call to grow in courage:

> For God did not give us a spirit of timidity, but a spirit of power, of love and of self-discipline.
>
> *2 Timothy 1:7*

DISCIPLINE

REFLECTIONS FROM SESSION 1

1. Describe a fear you have been confronting and dealing with since your last meeting.
2. If you took time to memorize 2 Timothy 1:7, communicate what this passage has taught you about courage.

THE BIG PICTURE

If you had the opportunity to examine people who have experienced a measure of success in their lives, I think you would find that discipline played a significant role in almost every instance. On the other hand, if you reviewed the history of people who have experienced a string of setbacks and failures, they would probably offer you a very candid picture of why so many calamities have befallen them. You might hear them say things like, "I just started to let things slide. I got overconfident. I stopped doing my homework. I didn't keep my eye on the store. I didn't take care of myself. I thought problems would solve themselves." The list would go on and on. All of these phrases stem from what we could call a lack of discipline.

This is not to say all disciplined people succeed and all those who struggle to succeed are undisciplined. I am simply making the observation that often discipline leads to noticeably positive results and a lack of discipline almost always undermines dreams and goals. If you think about it, discipline is one of the most important character qualities a person can possess.

A WIDE ANGLE VIEW

1 Mark where you feel you are on this continuum in each of the following areas:

Spiritual discipline (Personal time with God, attending worship, serving Christ . . .)

|———————————————————————————|

| very | slightly | disciplined | highly |
| undisciplined | disciplined | | disciplined |

Physical discipline (Eating habits, exercise, sleep habits, care for your body . . .)

|———————————————————————————|

| very | slightly | disciplined | highly |
| undisciplined | disciplined | | disciplined |

Financial discipline (Using money wisely, paying bills on time, saving responsibly . . .)

|———————————————————————————|

| very | slightly | disciplined | highly |
| undisciplined | disciplined | | disciplined |

Relational Discipline (Spending time communicating, being honest, keeping appointments . . .)

|———————————————————————————|

| very | slightly | disciplined | highly |
| undisciplined | disciplined | | disciplined |

In which area are you strongest?

What do you think helps you stay strong in this area of discipline?

In which area do you need to grow the most?

A BIBLICAL PORTRAIT

Read Proverbs 1:1–7

2 What characteristics mark the life of a person who is growing in wisdom?

How does Proverbs connect discipline and wisdom?

3 How would the writer of Proverbs respond to these two statements:

- A disciplined person is a wise person!

- An undisciplined person is a fool!

Read Snapshot "The Essence of Discipline . . . Delayed Gratification"

THE ESSENCE OF DISCIPLINE . . .
DELAYED GRATIFICATION

What is the essence of discipline? A good two-word explanation of this illusive character quality might be *delayed gratification*.

Delayed gratification is the commitment to schedule the pain of life first so we can really experience the pleasures of life that follow. We endure the pain of daily exercise for the satisfaction of a healthy body. We roll out of a warm bed fifteen minutes earlier in the morning for the joy of spending time quietly before God. We keep a strict budget so we can save up for that family vacation. We endure the chaos of honest, heart-to-heart talks with close friends because we know this is the only way to build authentic relationships. In every area of life, discipline begins with delayed gratification.

---

4 What would delayed gratification look like in *one* of these areas of your life:

- Spiritually committing yourself to deeper growth
- Physically getting in better shape
- Financially planning responsibly for the future
- Relationally growing closer to a specific person in your life

5 What is standing in the way of you exercising discipline in this area?

What can you do to remove this obstacle?

Read Snapshot "The Practice of Discipline . . . Advanced Decision-Making"

THE PRACTICE OF DISCIPLINE . . .
ADVANCED DECISION-MAKING

Understanding discipline and practicing it are two different things. The key to the practice of discipline can be described in two words: *advanced decision-making.* Once you make up your mind that the only decent way to live is to schedule the pain of life first, then you must go the next step and make advanced decisions as to how you are going to practice discipline in the various dimensions of your life. This involves things like setting a specific time each day to exercise, establishing a habit of taking time for prayer and study of the Bible, committing a specific amount of money from each paycheck to go into savings or investments, setting a date night with your spouse on a regular basis, and other measurable commitments. In short, make advanced decisions about how to live your life and then stand by your commitments.

---

6 What advanced, specific, measurable decisions will you have to make if you are going to exercise discipline in the following areas of your life (discuss one):

- Your spiritual life
- Your physical health
- Your personal finances
- One specific relationship

7 What specific aspects of your struggle would you like group members to pray for in the coming weeks?

Read Snapshot "The Rewards of Discipline"

THE REWARDS OF DISCIPLINE

A disciplined life yields reward after reward after reward. The payoff for spiritual discipline is a stable, mature Christian life, one of satisfaction, contentedness, and an availability to God. The payoff for relational discipline is a flourishing marriage and family life, a network of significant relationships, and intimate friendships with other followers of Christ. The payoff for physical discipline is a fit body, increased energy, resistance to sickness, lower insurance rates, higher concentration levels, and increased self-worth. The payoff for financial discipline is freedom from the bondage of debt as well as the satisfaction of knowing you have a little nest egg growing. It all begins with delaying gratification.

8
What are some of the rewards you have experienced when you have exercised discipline in your life?

PUTTING YOURSELF IN THE PICTURE

A PLAN FOR DEVELOPING DISCIPLINE

Take time in the coming month to set personal goals for growing in discipline in one specific area of your life. Use the three-step process from this study as a guideline for growing in discipline.

The area I want to grow in discipline is:

_____

Step 1: Delayed Gratification

What are some of the pleasures you may have to delay or set aside if you are going to exercise discipline in this area of your life? What are some of the risks or pains you may have to endure as you grow in discipline? Be very honest about these and pray for God's strength.

Step 2: Advanced Decision-Making

What specific and measurable goals are you going to have to set if you are going to be disciplined in this area? What do you have to start doing? When will you do it? How often? For how long? What must you stop doing? Who will pray for you and keep you accountable? Be as specific as possible.

Step 3: Rejoicing in the Rewards

When you begin to see the fruit of your labors and to experience the rewards of discipline, rejoice and thank God for His plan for your life. Remember the words of Solomon in the first chapter of Proverbs and thank God for His wise plan for your life. Let this time of celebration move you into a deeper examination of other areas of your life where you need to grow deeper in discipline.

CONFIDENCE

REFLECTIONS FROM SESSION 2

1. In which area of your life have you been seeking to develop discipline since your last group meeting? How has a deeper level of discipline in this area impacted your life?

THE BIG PICTURE

Picture 250 eight- to ten-year-old little boys in swimming trunks all standing in a line by the waterfront of a summer camp. It's the first day of a two-week camp experience, and they are about ready to take the mandatory swimming test. The test is simple: Each camper has to walk out on the pier, jump into the water, and swim approximately twenty-five yards to the next pier. Each swimmer who makes it to the other pier receives a brightly colored bead on a fishing-line necklace that will hang around his neck for the next two weeks. If the kid does a really good job swimming he'll get a green bead, which means he can swim anywhere. If he does a moderately good job, he will get a yellow bead. This means there will be a few restrictions in where he can swim. If a kid barely makes it to the other pier, he gets a red bead. There are many restrictions where he can swim, but he is given some freedom to enjoy the water.

The ten to fifteen boys who fail to swim the twenty-five yards receive a small lead weight. For the next two weeks they will be known by everyone else in camp as the "sinkers." For the next two weeks the boys with green, yellow, and even red beads will make sure their necklaces hang on the outside of their T-shirts, while the little guys with the sinkers will do their best to keep their necklaces with the lead weights hidden from view. Wouldn't you?

Every morning for the next two weeks the campers take swimming lessons. They are grouped together by the color of the bead hanging around their necks. The hope is that every boy will be able to improve at least one level in the two-week camping period. I was a swimming instructor at the camp where this system of teaching was used. My favorite group to teach was the sinkers.

Let me tell you, swimming class was not much fun for sinkers. Their confidence level was at rock bottom! I'd begin the lesson by saying, "How many of you would like to rip that sinker off your neck and throw it into the middle of the lake?" Every hand would shoot up into the air. I'd say, "Well, I'm going to see to it that all of you are going to have that opportunity some time in the next two weeks. In fact, I'm going to make it my goal to make sure every one of you can make it from the pier where you're sitting all the way over to the other pier without touching bottom. And when you crawl up the ladder on that other pier, the first thing I want you to do is grab hold of that fishing line, rip it off your neck, and throw it as far as you can."

Then one of the little guys would raise his hand and say, "But Bill, we can't swim!" And another little guy would say, "My dad told me I'm too skinny to swim!" Another one would say, "My mom said I'm too young to swim!" And another would say, "My older brother says I'm too dumb to swim!"

"What do they know?" I assured them.

After doing all I could to build their confidence, I would start teaching them to swim. We began by simply playing in the shallow water to get used to it. Next, I taught them to float on their backs. I would suggest that if they could float long enough, maybe a good breeze might push them to the other pier. Then I had them start moving their hands like little paddles while they were floating on their backs. As soon as they discovered that they were moving, I could see in their eyes that they were thinking about ripping off that lead sinker and getting their red bead. With their confidence and momentum building, I would have them turn over onto their stomachs and learn a few very basic strokes. After a while, I could see that a number of the boys were starting to get it.

One by one I would have the boys try to make it from one pier to the other. As each one started swimming slowly across, I'd be in the water next to them cheering them on, with the boys already on the far pier screaming at the top of their lungs. You would have thought those boys were watching an Olympic event. Sometimes other swim classes would even take a break and come over to cheer for them.

Every time one of those little guys made it all the way across, he would climb out of the water and, with fire burning in his eyes, would rip that sinker off his neck and pitch it into the lake as far as he could. I never tired of seeing this birth of confidence.

A WIDE ANGLE VIEW

1

Tell your group about an area in which you lacked self-confidence as a child.

If you have overcome your lack of self-confidence in this area, what helped you gain confidence?

A BIBLICAL PORTRAIT

Read Psalm 139:1–14

2

This psalm gives us a window to see our relationship with God more clearly. What do you learn about God's relationship with you from this psalm?

3

In verse 14 we read these words, "I praise you because I am fearfully and wonderfully made; your works are wonderful, I know that full well." Finish this statement: I know I am fearfully and wonderfully made because . . .

SHARPENING THE FOCUS

Read Snapshot "Acknowledge the Presence of God-Given Potential"

ACKNOWLEDGE THE PRESENCE OF GOD-GIVEN POTENTIAL

When people stay locked into a self-doubting mind-set, God is deeply grieved. When someone says, "Everybody else was given talent, but I got passed over," I can almost hear God say in a thunderous tone, "Watch what you say! You are fearfully and wonderfully made. I made you Myself! You have a mind a thousand computers can't match. You are the crown of My creation. Stop saying you got shorted, because the truth is you are bursting with a variety of potential. You just have to learn how to develop what I put in you."

As a member of the human race, you are extraordinarily gifted for the mere reason that you were created in the image of an awesome God. The first step in developing self-confidence is acknowledging the presence of your God-given potential.

4 What is one ability, talent, or spiritual gift God has given you?

How have you developed and used it?

5 How have you seen one of your group members develop and use a God-given talent, ability, or gift?

Read Snapshot "Do Something!"

DO SOMETHING!

The second step in developing confidence is proving to yourself that you have God-given abilities that are begging to be developed. In order to do this, you're going to have to leave the safety and security of the comfort zone you live in so that you can learn something new.

This might mean signing up for a class that stretches you intellectually to prove to yourself that your mind functions well. Maybe you need to take private lessons in an area that will stretch your artistic or athletic skills. Or maybe you should become a part of a group activity or a new challenge at work or a ministry in your church.

You see, people who never leave their comfort zones don't grow in their confidence! You develop confidence by gritting your teeth and saying, "If I am fearfully made, and if I have all of this divine potential within me, I'm going to try something new and see what happens."

6

What is one God-given ability, talent, or spiritual gift that you need to develop and start using?

What can you do to start developing greater levels of competency in this area of your life?

Read Snapshot "Confidence Builders"

CONFIDENCE BUILDERS

We need to become "confidence builders" to one another. People in relationships with one another need to start saying to each other, "I believe in you. You have potential you haven't begun to tap into. I am excited to see what God is going to do in and through your life as you take risks and grow in confidence."

Parents need to inspire, challenge, and encourage their children to stretch so they grow in confidence. Spouses need to say to one another, "Honey, I believe you are a gifted person. Let's identify an area where you can take a risk. I'll be right by your side as you take on this challenge." Believers need to start stretching each other and challenging each other to take a confident step forward and be willing to take risks for the sake of growth.

7

What is one area in your life in which you need your small group members to pray for you and commit themselves to be confidence builders for you?

What are specific things they can say and do that would inspire you to take risks in this area?

8

Everyone needs a confidence builder in their life. Who is one person you will commit yourself to encourage and challenge to grow in confidence?

What will you do to be a confidence builder in this person's life?

PUTTING YOURSELF IN THE PICTURE

LIVING ON THE EDGE

Choose an area in your life in which you lack confidence. Do something that will build confidence. If you are afraid to sing in a group, take a voice lesson. If you are afraid of heights, ride in a glass elevator. If you can't pray out loud in a group, find a person who will pray one-on-one with you until you are ready to pray in a group. You get the point! Be specific, set a goal, live on the edge, and rejoice as you see confidence growing in your life.

A CONFIDENCE-BUILDING MISSION

Affirm and encourage people in your life who need to grow in confidence. Identify one person in each of the three areas listed below and set a practical goal for how you will encourage each of them to grow in confidence:

- A family member: _____

  What will you do to help build confidence in his or her life?

- A friend: _____

  What will you do to help build confidence in his or her life?

- A small group member: _____

  What will you do to help build confidence in his or her life?

PATIENCE

1. What have you been doing to actively build confidence in at least one area of your life since your last group meeting?
2. Describe your efforts to be a confidence builder in the life of another person. How has that person responded to your confidence-building efforts?

THE BIG PICTURE

Patience runs contrary to my temperament. It is the subject that I am most often told needs attention in my life. In fact, my wife doesn't even have to call this vice of impatience to my attention verbally any more. The other morning, as I stood tapping my finger on the counter waiting for our high-powered microwave to warm up a bran muffin and I said, "Come on, these things take forever!" Lynne just smiled and rolled her eyes. She can give me one look and I am reminded how I need to grow this character quality in my life.

Living near Chicago means I drive many roads that require paying tolls. One day I had a commitment to speak at a conference in downtown Chicago. I left the church a little late, so I was rushing. I was a little perturbed when I approached a toll booth near the O'Hare Airport and realized I didn't have exact change. Quickly, I made a bold three-lane traverse to get to the shortest line with an attendant.

Wouldn't you know it? The guy in front of me didn't have the measly forty cents to pay the toll. Do you know what happens when you can't afford to pay the toll? The attendant has to close up the booth while he finds the official form, sharpens a pencil, walks out in front of the car, writes down the license number, and hands the form on a clipboard to the driver. Then the driver has to write down his name, address, phone number, social security number, home bank, political party affiliation, and the names of all family members including second cousins twice removed! Well, at least some of that information. I was boxed in and couldn't change lanes. I thought about jumping out and paying the forty cents, but the guy was in a really expensive car and I was getting a demented kind of satisfaction out of watching the drama unfold. I was tempted to honk and point, "He can make the payments, but he can't afford the tolls!"

In those kinds of moments—and we have all had them— don't you wish you could take a pill that would immediately give you patience? Of course the pills would have to work fast . . . impatient people don't want a slow-acting pill. But if you could develop a fast-acting patience pill, you would make a million dollars. I know I would buy stock in that company.

A WIDE ANGLE VIEW

1 What are some of the moments in your life when you wish you could take a patience pill?

A BIBLICAL PORTRAIT

Read Luke 15:11–24

2 If you had been the father in this story, what are some of the possible responses you would have had to your son when he finally returned home?

3 Describe the father in this story in one sentence.

How does this story communicate God's incredible patience toward us?

SHARPENING THE FOCUS

Read Snapshot "When Patience Runs Out, Watch Out!"

WHEN PATIENCE RUNS OUT, WATCH OUT!

When patience runs out and a husband launches a verbal attack on his wife, he wounds her. Later he hopes that she'll forget those words, but she can't because they've been registered in her memory bank and burned on her heart. The same thing happens when a wife gives her husband a "you're pathetic" look that cuts deeper than words. Or when an exasperated father says to his little boy, "Look, just hit the ball, will you? All the other kids your age can hit the ball. What's wrong with you?" Or when a mother says to her daughter, "Just get out of the kitchen. All you're capable of doing is making a mess." Or when an employer says to an employee, "Why do I even pay you? I can do better than that. Get out of my way."

When patience wears thin, the pastor says to the congregation, "Nobody around here is committed like I am." And the congregation says to its pastor, "Where did you learn to preach, anyway?" When patience runs out, watch out! Someone is going to get hurt.

---

4 Tell about a time someone launched a verbal attack on you.

If that person had been patient, how could that moment in your personal history been different?

In a small group of two or three, take a moment to pray for each other. Pray for healing in the lives of those who have experienced pain or hurt at the hands of someone who was impatient with them. Next, allow a time for confession and forgiveness of the times you have hurt others through your impatience.

Read Snapshot "God's Patience with Unbelievers"

GOD'S PATIENCE WITH UNBELIEVERS

As you grow in your knowledge of God and the Bible, you will be struck with the depth of God's patience toward rebellious, sinful, pride-filled people. The beginning chapters of Genesis all the way through the book of Revelation contain record after record of human rebellion and running from God. As a righteous and holy God, He could have eliminated all offenders—exterminated the entire race. However, God still loves His children and seeks to enter into a love relationship with them.

In Psalm 103:8 we read these words, "The LORD is compassionate and gracious, slow to anger, abounding in love." Other passages call Him a long-suffering God. When we remember His patience with us and with all who are still running from Him, we are called to share in the same loving patience God shows.

---

5 Before you were a follower of Christ, God extended great patience toward you. Describe how God was patient with you in *one* of these areas:

- How you treated family members
- How you used your words
- How you acted in the workplace
- How you viewed God and how you spoke of Him

Read Snapshot "God's Patience with Believers"

GOD'S PATIENCE WITH BELIEVERS

 God was not only patient with you before you were a follower of Christ, but He has been patient with you every day since you became a Christian. When I think of God's patience with believers, I think of the apostle Peter. I'm always amazed at how Peter tried the patience of Jesus, and how Jesus just kept on loving him. One minute Peter would say, "You are the Christ. The Son of the living God. I'll die for you," and then the next minute, he would say, "Jesus who? I don't know the man!" One minute he would be walking on water, and the next he would be drowning in doubt and fear. In the midst of all of this, Jesus put up with Peter—a picture of inconsistency.

God grows patience in our lives as we see His great patience with us. When we picture how long-suffering and patient God has been with us it seems to just melt away our impatience. God slowly softens our hard hearts and quietly replaces them with an attitude of tolerance, understanding, and forbearance.

---

6 God showed patience with Peter in the middle of all his inconsistency. What is one inconsistent area of your life in which God is extending patience today?

What needs to happen for you to grow more consistent in this area?

7 What is one situation in your life in which you are struggling with impatience?

How can your group members support you as you seek to yield to the supernatural power of the Holy Spirit by being patient in this situation?

Learning from a Patient Father

The story in Luke 15:11–24 is often called "The Parable of the Prodigal Son." It might be more appropriately titled, "The Parable of the Patient Father." In this story God is the Father, and He is patient beyond our wildest imagination.

Take time in the coming week to identify one or two situations in which you tend to get impatient. Imagine God, your patient heavenly Father, walking into each situation. How would He respond? What attitude would He bring? As you picture His responses, pray for strength to enter these situations with a new spirit of patience that reflects the heart of your heavenly Father.

Honest Confession

If there is a person you have been impatient with in the past, contact that person and admit your impatience. Let him or her know God is working on this character trait in your life and that you will be seeking to live with a deeper level of patience in the future. If this person is a believer, ask him or her to pray for you as you grow in this area.

ENDURANCE

REFLECTIONS FROM SESSION 4

1. How has focusing on God as your patient heavenly Father helped you develop the characteristic of patience in your life?

2. If you contacted someone and asked for forgiveness for your impatience in the past, how did the person respond? What impact has this had on your relationship?

THE BIG PICTURE

If you were to take an inventory of your life history, what is one thing you wish you hadn't quit? You might say, "I wish I had never quit high school or college. Boy, I wish I had stuck with it through graduation day." Or maybe you look back and wish you would have finished those dance lessons, that skiing program, or the pottery class you always said you would get back to once things "slowed down."

You might have to be honest and say, "I wish I hadn't quit working on my relationship in my first marriage. I gave up somewhere along the way." Or, "I wish I hadn't quit working on a friendship that dissolved some years ago. Now I live with scars, detachment, and alienation."

You might even be saying, "I wish I hadn't come to the point where I stopped asking spiritual questions and struggling with eternal issues. I wish I hadn't thrown in the towel spiritually and quit on God."

Scripture advises us not to live in the past. But occasionally it pays to consider the high cost of quitting. Too many people live with scars from having quit on someone or something. They look back on their lives and say, "Why did I cash in so easily? Why did I cop out when I should have hung in? Why didn't I endure through the hard times?"

I think the answer is obvious: *It is infinitely easier to quit than to endure.* There's no magic about that answer. It is easier to not go to lessons than to keep going week after week. It is easier to roll over in bed than to get up early and go to work. It is easier to walk out of a room during an argument with your spouse than to stay and work through the conflict. It is easier to read the paper and drink your cup of coffee in the family room than it is to wake up the family, get everyone dressed, and drive to church every week. It's just easier to quit.

A WIDE ANGLE VIEW

1   As you look back over your life, what is one thing you wish you wouldn't have quit?

A BIBLICAL PORTRAIT

Read James 1:2–4, 12

2   In this passage, James walks us through a process of growing in maturity? What are the elements of this process?

Why is endurance an essential part of this process?

3

James invites us to "consider it pure joy" when we face struggles that demand endurance. This seems an unlikely attitude for people facing trials and difficult times. How is it possible to experience deep joy while persevering through a difficult experience?

SHARPENING THE FOCUS

Read Snapshot "Identifying Quitting Points"

IDENTIFYING QUITTING POINTS

Runners know what a quitting point is. You hit it like a brick wall on the twentieth lap when your sides are splitting, your legs are heavy, your throat is burning, and all that occupies your mind is a desire to quit. It's the point at which your heart, mind, and body cry out, "Quit. That's it. Enough. Not one more lap. Not one more half lap. Not one more step. STOP!"

It happens when the pressure is mounting and the deadline is drawing near. You're working as hard as you know how and the boss comes in and barks out one more assignment. In your mind you say, "That's it. I can't stand it one moment longer. All I can think about is writing a resignation notice and throwing it on my boss's desk."

It's when you're in the middle of that familiar argument with your spouse about the same old thing. You've been going back and forth and you see no resolution in sight. Frustration is growing by the minute, and your spouse says all the words that just push your buttons. You feel your emotions going through the roof. Everything inside of you says, "Quit. Storm out. Move out. Leave. It's not worth it anymore." That's a quitting point.

4

Choose an area below and identify some of the quitting points you face:

- Physically
- Relationally
- Morally
- Educationally
- Spiritually
- Professionally

5 What is a critical quitting point you are facing in your life right now?

What is pushing you to the point of quitting?

Read Snapshot "Crashing Through Quitting Points"

CRASHING THROUGH QUITTING POINTS

Quitting points are not made of stone; they are made of tissue paper! If we are going to develop the character of endurance in our lives, we need to learn how to press on and crash through those quitting points we think are impenetrable.

When long-distance runners hit the "wall" and feel they can't go another step, they press on and discover that the quitting point was only made of tissue paper . . . they endure. People who want to quit their jobs again and again break through and discover they *can* do it after all. Spouses who want more than anything to walk out and never come back crash through and discover real communication, intimacy, and joy.

When it comes to quitting points, we need to draw on God's strength and crash through them. This is the key to learning endurance. We might not feel a lot of slaps on the back in those moments, we may not hear angels singing or see the spotlights of heaven, but in our spirit we hear the words, "Blessed are those who draw on God's strength and endure through trials and crash through quitting points."

6 Tell about a time you endured and crashed through a quitting point in your life.

What did it take to persevere to the point of breaking through this quitting point?

How did it feel to crash through this quitting point?

7 Respond to this statement: "Almost every quitting point we face *looks* like an impenetrable brick wall. After we crash through it we discover it was a facade . . . it was really made of tissue paper."

Read Snapshot "Developing Endurance"

DEVELOPING ENDURANCE

Once we begin crashing through quitting points, we must commit ourselves to developing endurance in every area of our lives. This involves establishing a pattern of always pushing ourselves a little beyond where we feel comfortable. I like to run an extra lap after I have finished my workout just to push the endurance envelope. When I have finished a sermon and feel like I have studied and prayed all I can, I try to take one more half hour and give it just a little more work. When I go out wind-surfing and my arms are burning, I like to turn away from shore one more time and challenge my endurance level. Developing endurance is a choice that should become a lifestyle for all of us.

---

8 What is one specific area in which you want to develop endurance in your life?

How can your small group members be a support as you develop endurance in this area?

PUTTING YOURSELF IN THE PICTURE

Exercising Endurance

- Identify one specific area in your life in which you have a pattern of quitting. What are the barriers that stand in your way? What tends to lead up to the point of caving in?
- Crash through the quitting point you have identified. What is it going to take to break through this point? Once you break through it, write down how you felt and what you found on the other side.
- Develop endurance in the area you identified. Once you have broken through your quitting point, take additional steps of endurance on a daily basis in this area of your life. It is always wise to have one or more people praying for you and encouraging you along the way.

Scripture Memory

Take time in the coming week to memorize this passage and to reflect on what it means to you:

> Blessed is the man who perseveres under trial, because when he has stood the test, he will receive the crown of life that God has promised to those who love him.
>
> *James 1:12*

CONTENTMENT

REFLECTIONS FROM SESSION 5

1. If you were able to crash through a quitting point since your last small group meeting, describe this experience to your group.
2. If you memorized James 1:12, tell your group how this passage has challenged you to live with a deeper level of endurance.

THE BIG PICTURE

All he really wanted in life was *more*. He wanted more money, so he parlayed his inherited wealth into a billion-dollar pile of assets. He wanted more fame, so he broke into the Hollywood scene and became a filmmaker and star. He wanted more sensual pleasures from women, so he paid handsome sums of money to indulge his every sexual urge. He wanted more thrills, so he designed, built, and piloted the fastest aircraft in the world. He wanted more power, so he secretly dealt political favors so skillfully that two U.S. presidents became his pawns.

All he ever really wanted was more. You see, he was absolutely convinced that more would bring him happiness. Unfortunately, history shows otherwise. Here is a brief chronicle of the last days of this man's life:

> He was emaciated, practically skeletal, with only 120 pounds stretched over his six-foot, four-inch frame. There was hardly a speck of color anywhere on his body, even in his lips. He was not dead, but it seemed his body was already in decay. Only the long grey hair that trailed halfway down his back, the thin straggly beard that reached midway onto his sunken chest, and his hideously long nails that extended several inches in grotesque yellow corkscrews from his fingers and toes seemed to still be growing, still showing signs of life. Then there were his eyes. Near the end of his life they often looked dead blank, but other times they gleamed from their deep-sunk sockets with surprising, almost frightening intensity. Many of his teeth were rotting black stumps. A tumor was emerging from

the side of his head, a reddened lump protruding from his sparse strands of grey hair. His bed sores festered all the way down his back, some so severe that eventually one shoulder bone poked through his parchment-like skin. Then there were the needle marks. The telltale tracks ran the full length of both his thin arms, scarred his thighs, and clustered horribly around his groin.

The man's name was Howard Hughes, and he died a billionaire junkie. He banked his whole life on the lie that unbridled pursuit of more leads to gladness. In his death we learn that it actually leads to madness.

A WIDE ANGLE VIEW

1   Describe some of the consequences you have seen arise in the lives of people who can't ever seem to say, "Enough!"

A BIBLICAL PORTRAIT

Read Psalm 103:1–13

2   According to this psalm, what does God provide for His children?

How have you experienced the truth of this psalm in your life?

3

After reading this psalm closely, describe the heart and character of God.

How does a discontent person who is always seeking more look in the light of this picture of God?

SHARPENING THE FOCUS

Read Snapshot "The Myth of More"

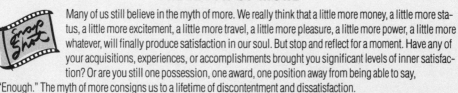

THE MYTH OF MORE

Many of us still believe in the myth of more. We really think that a little more money, a little more status, a little more excitement, a little more travel, a little more pleasure, a little more power, a little more whatever, will finally produce satisfaction in our soul. But stop and reflect for a moment. Have any of your acquisitions, experiences, or accomplishments brought you significant levels of inner satisfaction? Or are you still one possession, one award, one position away from being able to say, "Enough." The myth of more consigns us to a lifetime of discontentment and dissatisfaction.

4

What fuels this constant surge of discontentedness in people's hearts and lives?

5

How have you seen yourself believing this myth?

Read Snapshot "Emptiness of Soul"

EMPTINESS OF SOUL

Saint Augustine said, "Our human hearts are restless until they find their rest in God." What was he saying? The very same thing Jesus said to His listeners in a dozen different ways; that human beings have a God-shaped vacuum that only a living relationship with their Creator can fill. When this void remains open, we spend much of our time and energy trying to fill it. We live with a deep sense of discontent and nothing seems to satisfy. No matter how much we get, it never seems to be enough. What so few realize is that the problem is not our lack of *things*, the problem is that our soul is empty and hungers for God.

6 Describe what your life was like before you knew the love and forgiveness of Jesus.

What were some of the things with which you tried to fill the void in your heart?

7 Is there someone in your life who still has an empty soul and needs to know the love of God? Who is that person?

How can your small group members encourage you to reach out to this person with the love of God?

Read Snapshot "Fullness of Soul"

FULLNESS OF SOUL

The first step to finding fullness of soul is when a person realizes their sin has separated them from God. Then, when they realize only Jesus Christ can forgive their sin and reconcile them to the Father, they have to make an eternal decision. When they fall to the floor and cry out, "I am a sinner and am separated from God! I need to be cleansed and forgiven and reconciled to God!" Jesus Christ answers their cry for help. They receive reconciliation, forgiveness, and cleansing. The presence of God floods their soul and they receive salvation. They are adopted into the family of God and Christ miraculously fills their empty soul. The vacuum is filled. Yearning and the restlessness cease. A new life begins.

8 How has your life changed since the void in your heart has been filled with the presence of God?

PUTTING YOURSELF IN THE PICTURE

A Full Heart Is a Thankful Heart

Take time in the coming days to thank God for entering your heart and life. Thank Him for meeting your needs, forgiving your sins, giving you new life, and adopting you as His child. Let the fullness of your heart overflow in expressions of thankfulness. It might help to read Psalm 103, which focuses on many areas of God's provision in our lives.

Giving Away What We Have

If you have Christ living in your heart, you are filled to overflowing. You have everything you need. With this in mind, pray for courage to develop a lifestyle of giving. Find practical ways to give in the following areas: (1) telling others about God's love; (2) financially; (3) your time; and (4) a listening ear.

Leader's Notes

Leading a Bible discussion—especially for the first time—can make you feel both nervous and excited. If you are nervous, realize that you are in good company. Many biblical leaders, such as Moses, Joshua, and the apostle Paul, felt nervous and inadequate to lead others (see, for example, 1 Cor. 2:3). Yet God's grace was sufficient for them, just as it will be for you.

Some excitement is also natural. Your leadership is a gift to the others in the group. Keep in mind, however, that other group members also share responsibility for the group. Your role is simply to stimulate discussion by asking questions and encouraging people to respond. The suggestions listed below can help you to be an effective leader.

Preparing to Lead

1. Ask God to help you understand and apply the passage to your own life. Unless that happens, you will not be prepared to lead others.
2. Carefully work through each question in the study guide. Meditate and reflect on the passage as you formulate your answers.
3. Familiarize yourself with the Leader's Notes for each session. These will help you understand the purpose of the session and will provide valuable information about the questions in the session. The Leader's Notes are not intended to be read to the group. These notes are primarily for your use as a group leader and for your preparation. However, when you find a section that relates well to your group, you may want to read a brief portion or encourage them to read this section at another time.
4. Pray for the various members of the group. Ask God to use these sessions to make you better disciples of Jesus Christ.
5. Before the first session, make sure each person has a study guide. Encourage them to prepare beforehand for each session.

Leading the Session

1. Begin the session on time. If people realize that the session begins on schedule, they will work harder to arrive on time.

2. At the beginning of your first time together, explain that these sessions are designed to be discussions, not lectures. Encourage everyone to participate, but realize some may be hesitant to speak during the first few sessions.

3. Don't be afraid of silence. People in the group may need time to think before responding.

4. Avoid answering your own questions. If necessary, rephrase a question until it is clearly understood. Even an eager group will quickly become passive and silent if they think the leader will do most of the talking.

5. Encourage more than one answer to each question. Ask, "What do the rest of you think?" or "Anyone else?" until several people have had a chance to respond.

6. Try to be affirming whenever possible. Let people know you appreciate their insights into the passage.

7. Never reject an answer. If it is clearly wrong, ask, "Which verse led you to that conclusion?" Or let the group handle the problem by asking them what they think about the question.

8. Avoid going off on tangents. If people wander off course, gently bring them back to the passage being considered.

9. Conclude your time together with conversational prayer. Ask God to help you apply those things that you learned in the session.

10. End on time. This will be easier if you control the pace of the discussion by not spending too much time on some questions or too little on others.

We encourage all small group leaders to use *Leading Life-Changing Small Groups* (Zondervan) by Bill Donahue and the Willow Creek Small Group Team while leading their group. Developed and used by Willow Creek Community Church, this guide is an excellent resource for training and equipping followers of Christ to effectively lead small groups. It includes valuable information on how to utilize fun and creative relationship-building exercises for your group; how to plan your meeting; how to share the leadership load by identifying, developing, and working with an "apprentice leader"; and how to find creative ways to do group prayer. In addition, the book includes material and tips on handling potential conflicts and difficult personalities, forming group covenants, inviting new members, improving listening skills, studying the Bible, and much more. Using *Leading Life-Changing Small Groups* will help you create a group that members love to be a part of.

Now let's discuss the different elements of this small group study guide and how to use them for the session portion of your group meeting.

THE BIG PICTURE

Each session will begin with a short story or overview of the lesson theme. This is called "The Big Picture" because it introduces the central theme of the session. You will need to read this section as a group or have group members read it on their own before discussion begins. Here are three ways you can approach this section of the small group session:

- As the group leader, read this section out loud for the whole group and then move into the questions in the next section, "A Wide Angle View." (You might read the first week, but then use the other two options below to encourage group involvement.)
- Ask a group member to volunteer to read this section for the group. This allows another group member to participate. It is best to ask someone in advance to give them time to read over the section before reading it to the group. It is also good to ask someone to volunteer, and not to assign this task. Some people do not feel comfortable reading in front of a group. After a group member has read this section out loud, move into the discussion questions.
- Allow time at the beginning of the session for each person to read this section silently. If you do this, be sure to allow enough time for everyone to finish reading so they can think about what they've read and be ready for meaningful discussion.

A WIDE ANGLE VIEW

This section includes one or more questions that move the group into a general discussion of the session topic. These questions are designed to help group members begin discussing the topic in an open and honest manner. Once the topic of the lesson has been established, move on to the Bible passage for the session.

A BIBLICAL PORTRAIT

This portion of the session includes a Scripture reading and one or more questions that help group members see how the theme of the session is rooted and based in biblical teaching. The Scripture reading can be handled just like "The Big Picture" section: You can read it for the group, have a group member read it, or allow time for silent reading. Make sure everyone has a Bible or that you have Bibles available for those who need them. Once you have read the passage, ask the question(s) in this section so that group members can dig into the truth of the Bible.

SHARPENING THE FOCUS

The majority of the discussion questions for the session are in this section. These questions are practical and help group members apply biblical teaching to their daily lives.

SNAPSHOTS

The "Snapshots" in each session help prepare group members for discussion. These anecdotes give additional insight to the topic being discussed. Each "Snapshot" should be read at a designated point in the session. This is clearly marked in the session as well as in theLeader's Notes. Again, follow the same format as you do with "The Big Picture" section and the "Biblical Portrait" section: Either you read the anecdote, have a group member volunteer to read, or provide time for silent reading. However you approach this section, you will find these anecdotes very helpful in triggering lively dialogue and moving discussion in a meaningful direction.

PUTTING YOURSELF IN THE PICTURE

Here's where you roll up your sleeves and put the truth into action. This portion is very practical and action-oriented. At the end of each session there will be suggestions for one or two ways group members can put what they've just learned into practice. Review the action goals at the end of each session and challenge group members to work on one or more of them in the coming week.

You will find follow-up questions for the "Putting Yourself in the Picture" section at the beginning of the next week's session. Starting with the second week, there will be time set aside at the beginning of the session to look back and talk about how you have tried to apply God's Word in your life since your last time together.

PRAYER

You will want to open and close your small group with a time of prayer. Occasionally, there will be specific direction within a session for how you can do this. Most of the time, however, you will need to decide the best place to stop and pray. You may want to pray or have a group member volunteer to begin the lesson with a prayer. Or you might want to read "The Big Picture" and discuss the "Wide Angle View" questions before opening in prayer. In some cases, it might be best to open in prayer after you have read the Bible passage. You need to decide where you feel an opening prayer best fits for your group.

When opening in prayer, think in terms of the session theme and pray for group members (including yourself) to be responsive to the truth of Scripture and the working of the Holy Spirit. If you have seekers in your group (people investigating Christianity but not yet believers), be sensitive to your expectations for group prayer. Seekers may not yet be ready to take part in group prayer.

Be sure to close your group with a time of prayer as well. One option is for you to pray for the entire group. Or you might allow time for group members to offer audible prayers that others can agree with in their hearts. Another approach would be to allow a time of silence for one-on-one prayers with God and then to close this time with a simple "Amen."

COURAGE

2 TIMOTHY 1:7–12

INTRODUCTION

The older I get, the more I understand how much courage it takes to face the ordinary challenges of life. We either choose to do the right thing or the easy and convenient thing. We either choose to stick to a conviction or cave in to compromise for the sake of comfort, greed, or approval. We either choose to take a risk or crawl into a shrinking shell of safety. Every day we make choices to either believe in God and trust Him—even when we don't understand His ways—or second-guess God and hide in corners of doubt and fear. This session concentrates on helping us learn to reclaim the endangered character quality of courage.

THE BIG PICTURE

Take time to read this introduction with the group. There are suggestions for how this can be done in the beginning of the leader's section.

A WIDE ANGLE VIEW

Question One Most of us have witnessed at least one act of amazing courage in our lifetime. After allowing time for group members to tell these stories, allow the focus to move toward the everyday accounts of courage we all witness. The focus of this study is not so much on the once-in-a-lifetime opportunities to show courage, but on the courage it takes every day to live as a fully devoted follower of Christ in a world that constantly calls us to cave in and compromise.

A BIBLICAL PORTRAIT

Read 2 Timothy 1:7–12

Questions Two & Three This passage reveals God's heart in the matter of courage and cowardice. God does not want spineless followers. There are too many cowards around these days. God says in His Word, "I have infused you with a spirit of power. A spirit of positive love. A spirit of competency." In other words, God has called us to courage.

It seems that the only time we hear about courage is when someone drags a person out of a burning building, dives into an icy pond to save a child, risks taking a bullet to pull someone out of the line of fire, or performs some other act of extreme heroism. Don't get me wrong, I love hearing those stories; but they seem bigger than life. Those dramatic, once-in-a-lifetime experiences never seem to happen to ordinary folks.

God calls us to be courageous in the daily challenges and struggles we face. Every day we have dozens of chances to retreat to the "safe" ground of cowardice and timidity. We also have the opportunity to make daily choices to live with courage. Take time as a group to identify what timidity looks like in daily life and what can motivate us to live with courage.

SHARPENING THE FOCUS

Read Snapshot "Spiritual Courage" before Question 4

Questions Four & Five One of my greatest delights in life is talking with people one-on-one about Christianity. Every time God gives me that opportunity, I try to take advantage of it. When the time is right and God leads me, I have often spoken words that only a courageous heart is willing to hear and receive: "You have to repent before a holy God. You have to tell Him the truth about yourself. That you've lied. You've hurt people. You've cheated. You've been greedy, dishonest, self-centered, and maybe even unfaithful to your spouse."

At that moment I see a vulnerability before a holy God that terrifies the person. Sometimes I notice people shift in their seats when I talk about repentance. Sometimes I see their eyes starting to move around the room, and I sense they are wondering how they're going to get out of the confrontation they are facing. The truth is, they are not concerned about me; they are fearful of coming face-to-face with a holy God.

Something inside of them is crying out, "Don't face it. Back off. Go with the flow. Get out of this confrontation. Don't look at yourself for who you really are. Cover your tracks." Sadly, too many people cave in to their fears and act cowardly. They say, "I just can't do it. It would be too embarrassing. It would make me too vulnerable. It would be too humiliating to speak the truth to a holy God about who I really am." And so they begin to say ridiculous things like, "Who? Me? Sin? Never! I've been a pretty good person. If there is a heaven, God would be glad to have me there. I might have made a few minor mistakes in judgment, but nobody is perfect."

When I hear that stuff, I often have the urge to just say, "You know what the right thing to do is but you're too chicken to do it. You don't have the guts to speak the truth to God about who you really are. You're afraid of the pain, the embarrassment, and the discomfort. You don't have the courage it takes to stand before God and admit you are a moral failure!"

Then I feel like saying, "If you're not going to admit the obvious—if you're too chicken to repent and own up before a holy God—then please don't ever parrot that statement, 'Christianity is for weak people.' Because, apparently, it's for people with more courage than you have." You see, to become a Christian you have to have courage to speak the truth to God and repent. Everyone who is a follower of Christ has come to the point where they have said, "I'm a sinful person. I often choose self over others, pleasure over service, greed over sharing, disobedience over obedience. I know what the right thing to do is, and *I don't do it*. I confess my sin and throw myself on the mercy of God." It takes incredible courage to become a Christian.

Read Snapshot "Moral Courage" before Question 6

Questions Six & Seven We live in a culture where moral courage is not only endangered, but practically extinct! Deceit, immorality, and duplicity run wild. When we choose to follow Christ, He calls us to live with moral courage even when no one else seems to care. Take time as a group to identify what moral courage looks like in some of the practical areas of our daily lives. Dare to ask each other to keep you accountable to live out lives of moral courage in the areas where you struggle the most.

Read Snapshot "Relational Courage" before Question 8

Questions Eight & Nine It takes courage to look your spouse in the eye and say, "We have serious trouble going on in this marriage, and we've got to do something about it." What do most people do? They go out in their own direction, pursuing their own career and their own recreation while their marriage disintegrates from lack of courage. They don't have the courage to say, "Let's go to a marriage retreat or see a marriage counselor. Let's get together with another couple we respect. Let's do our best to solve these problems." There are people who would run into a burning building or jump into a frozen lake before they would dare face the condition of their marriage.

And courage doesn't apply only to marriages. It takes relational courage to raise kids these days. How often I see parents backing off from proper discipline for their kids because they don't want to endure their kids' disapproval. The kids throw a tantrum or they say, "Mom or Dad, if you do such and such I'll hate you," and the parent backs off. As a parent, you have to manifest a little courage and say, "You can say whatever you want, but I know the right thing to do in this situation and I'm sticking by my convictions. I won't let you run over me." When I see little children intimidating their parents and those parents unwilling to summon the courage to stand up and raise that child the way God would have them to be raised, I see why we have a crisis on our hands. Where are parents who will manifest courage in raising their children?

It also takes relational courage to build significant relationships with brothers and sisters and friends. It takes courage to look a friend in the eye and say, "Isn't it time we stop talking about the weather, the stock market, and other surface issues and start talking about what's going on in our hearts and lives? Isn't it time we have the courage to build a deep friendship?" You will never be a relational success without courage.

PUTTING YOURSELF IN THE PICTURE

Tell group members you will be providing time at the beginning of the next meeting for them to discuss how they have put their faith into practice. Let them tell their stories. However, don't limit their interaction to the two options provided. They may have put themselves into the picture in some other way as a result of your study. Allow for honest and open communication.

Also, be clear that there will not be any kind of a "test" or forced reporting. All you are going to do is allow time for people to volunteer to talk about how they have implemented what they learned in your last study. Some group members will feel pressured if they think you are going to make everyone provide a "report." You don't want anyone to skip the next group because they are afraid of having to say they did not follow up on what they learned from the prior session. Focus instead on providing a place for honest communication without creating pressure or fear of being embarrassed.

Every session from this point on will open with a look back at the "Putting Yourself in the Picture" section of the previous session.

DISCIPLINE

PROVERBS 1:1—7

INTRODUCTION

Discipline is definitely an endangered character quality these days. It's not that people don't want to be disciplined; most of them actually have a deep desire to live disciplined lives. But very few are really sure what being disciplined means or how to attain such a seemingly lofty and illusive goal.

In this session we will look very closely at how we can grow in discipline. We will identify the essence, practice, and rewards of discipline. To make this very practical, I have identified four common areas in which people long to experience discipline in their lives: spiritual growth, physical fitness, personal finances, and developing deep and authentic relationships. Encourage each group member to identify one of these areas, or another specific area of concern in their life, and for them to keep their focus on this area throughout the study.

THE BIG PICTURE

Take time to read this introduction with the group. There are suggestions for how this can be done in the beginning of the leader's section.

A WIDE ANGLE VIEW

Question One This could be a very vulnerable moment for some group members. It is best to invite and encourage them to express where they are in their life—do not force every group member to respond to these questions. Some group members might not even feel comfortable marking where they fall on the continuum in the four areas of discipline. If this is the case, encourage them to make a mental mark on the page identifying where they see themselves in each area.

Expressing where we are doing well in personal discipline is just as important as identifying where we struggle. Use this opportunity to affirm and encourage those who are doing well in a specific area of personal discipline. Seek to create a safe climate where group members can honestly express where they need to be challenged to grow in discipline. Sim-

ply writing this down or expressing it out loud can mark the
beginning of a new area of growth toward personal maturity

A Biblical Portrait

Read Proverbs 1:1–7

Questions Two & Three Proverbs does not say that all
people who are disciplined are necessarily wise or that those
who lack discipline are always fools. However, it does make
some general observations about the critical place of discipline in the life of a person who wants to grow in wisdom.
The two statements in question three are not meant to reflect
the teaching of Proverbs as much as stir up good discussion
about what God is trying to communicate through this portion of the Bible.

Sharpening the Focus

Read Snapshot "The Essence of Discipline . . . Delayed Gratification" before Question 4

Questions Four & Five How can discipline affect your spiritual life? It's not uncommon for me to hear people say, "You
know, I've learned something over the years. If I would discipline myself to just spend five, ten, or fifteen minutes with
God early each morning, my life would be so much richer. If I
could only get away to a quiet place and write down some
thoughts, read my Bible, listen to a tape, sing some praise
songs, or pray, it would make all the difference in the world."
What are they saying? They're saying that by experiencing a
little discomfort and making a small investment of time, the
whole rest of their day would be better. This is delayed gratification as it pertains to our spiritual walk.

How about discipline as it pertains to your relational life?
Married couples who understand the value of discipline in
relationships say to each other, "Let's work very hard on this
marriage. Right now. Let's face our conflicts as they arise.
Let's work things out. Let's not let things slide. Let's do whatever it takes right now to make this marriage mutually satisfying." Why do they do this? So they can plan on brighter, more
fulfilling and satisfying days and years ahead. The same is true
when it comes to training up your children. If you devote
yourself to that impressionable era of the first ten years of a
child's life, you will discover the payoff lasts a lifetime.

What about discipline as it pertains to physical condition-
ing? People who understand delayed gratification make a

calculated decision to forego certain culinary ecstasies because they know that there will be a payoff at weigh-in time. The same is true of the pain experienced in rigorous exercise. When you exercise hard and give it all you have, there is a lingering satisfaction that lasts far into the night. You develop muscle tone, alertness, and an increased energy level. You feel better about yourself. The payoff comes after the hard work.

The same principal holds true in our financial lives. When a couple or an individual makes the conscious choice to do without something or not to spend some money so that they can put a little aside for a nest egg or a special vacation, the process of delayed gratification can be painful. However, when you see the savings grow or when you take that long-awaited trip, the benefits of discipline are rewarding.

Read Snapshot "The Practice of Discipline . . . Advanced Decision-Making" before Question 6

Questions Six & Seven I come from a family that has chronic heart problems on both sides. My two uncles on one side had heart attacks and died before they were fifty. I have five uncles on the other side who died of heart attacks before they were fifty. My own dad died at fifty-three. Saying this is a chronic problem in my family is no overstatement. Trouble first started showing up in my own heart when I was only fifteen, so I know what I need to do to take good care of my heart.

Mentally, I understand that I must first endure the pain of running and weight lifting if I'm going to experience the satisfaction or the payoff of feeling fit and being healthier. This means I must make advanced decisions to help me accomplish my goal. Theories and feelings won't do it. I need to be brutally honest and clear about what I am going to do each day if I am going to stay disciplined in this area of my life.

I have made an advanced decision that Monday through Friday I will leave the office at 3:30 P.M. and exercise. I write it on my calendar, and I am committed. The strange thing is, every day at about 3:15 my body starts sending signals to my mind. It says, "You don't want to work out today. You really, really don't want to work out. You're still a little sore from yesterday. You're busy in the ministry. You really don't want to exercise, do you?" Then I start thinking, *You know, I can skip a day. I don't want to be a fanatic. I deserve a little break.*

When it comes right down to that moment when all of those emotions and voices are converging, it is easy to cave in. But you see, in the practice of discipline, this thing called advanced decision-making says, "It's already been decided, so don't even think about it. These little signals don't change the fact that I have already made a decision and that it is non-negotiable."

When you determine what needs to happen on a regular basis for you to flourish in Christ, you harness the powers of discipline by making advanced decisions about your spiritual life. You say, "I'm making an advanced decision about being in church with God's people whenever they assemble. And I'm going to read my Bible, pray, journal, and spend time face-to-face with God every day. And I'm also going to find some like-minded Christians to fellowship with on a regular basis." These are commitments, decisions that are not up for grabs depending on how you feel at a given moment. Once you have made specific advanced decisions, it is much easier to follow through.

Read Snapshot "The Rewards of Discipline" before Question 8

PUTTING YOURSELF IN THE PICTURE

Challenge group members to take time in the coming week to use part or all of this application section as an opportunity for continued growth.

CONFIDENCE

PSALM 139:1—14

INTRODUCTION

When we talk about confidence, we're not talking about cockiness or haughtiness or arrogance. Instead, we're talking about a deep personal conviction that says, "I have some God-given gifts, skills, talents, and abilities, and I'm learning how to use them." Confidence is a growing awareness of personal competency that comes through challenging ourselves out of our comfort zone and being willing to grow in areas in which we never thought we could grow. It comes when we realize we are "fearfully and wonderfully made" in the image of God.

THE BIG PICTURE

Take time to read this introduction with the group. There are suggestions for how this can be done in the beginning of the leader's section.

A BIBLICAL PORTRAIT

Read Psalm 139:1–14

Questions Two & Three God created the heavens and the earth. He made the plants, animals, sun, moon, and stars. And as miraculous as that was, the Bible says God saved His best for last. In a dramatic display of power, He created a man and a woman—the most complex, sophisticated, miraculous, and mind-boggling manifestations of His greatness. Psalm 139 says that human beings are "fearfully and wonderfully made."

When God created human beings He gave us vast intellectual and incredible physical abilities. He filled us with so much ability, in fact, that we could not fully develop it in a hundred lifetimes. In addition, He made us in such a way that when we develop one of our God-given abilities, we are naturally filled with a surge of satisfaction. This gives us the unmistakable indication that God designed human beings with a desire and need to develop their God-given abilities and to become confident in them.

SHARPENING THE FOCUS

Read Snapshot "Acknowledge the Presence of God-Given Potential" before Question 4.

Read Snapshot "Do Something!" before Question 6

Question Six I have a daughter, Shauna, who is confident by temperament. Every single challenge I throw her way, she enthusiastically embraces. My son, Todd, has a different temperament. Ever since he was two or three years old, his standard response to every new opportunity was, "No, Dad, I could never do that." His temperament is more timid. "I could never learn how to ride a bike." "I could never learn how to use a skateboard." "I could never shoot a basketball and make one." "I could never learn how to catch a baseball." It's just the way he is wired.

Lynne and I have made it our personal goal to make sure we don't allow Todd to cave in to the temptation to always play it safe. I remember the first time Todd beat me in a motorcycle race. I missed one shift, went a little wide on a turn, and he cut inside and beat me to the finish line. When he skidded to the finish line, jumped off his motorcycle, and tore his helmet off, the look on his face was worth a million dollars to me. It was the same look I saw on the faces of those little "sinkers" who had finally made it over to the other pier, climbed up the ladder, broke the necklaces off their necks, and heaved them into the lake. He yelled, "I did it! I did it! I did it!"

What Todd was saying, in effect, was, "I've got some abilities. I've got some talents. I can do some things really well! Maybe I *am* fearfully and wonderfully made." This kind of confidence is contagious. When you take a risk, try something new, and succeed, confidence spills over into other areas. You begin to say, "I'll bet maybe with a little practice, a little training, and a little more effort, I could improve in this area." When this begins to happen, watch out!

Read Snapshot "Confidence Builders" before Question 7

Questions Seven & Eight God calls us to grow in confidence. He also gives us the awesome privilege of building others up in their confidence. Commit yourself to supporting the people in your life as they develop this vital character trait in their lives. Be willing to invite others to support you and encourage you as you grow in confidence.

Putting Yourself in the Picture

Challenge group members to take time in the coming week to use part or all of this application section as an opportunity for continued growth.

PATIENCE

LUKE 15:11—24

INTRODUCTION

Patience is another character quality on the top of many people's endangered list. We live in a world of microwave ovens, e-mail, and computers that seem to get faster on a daily basis. We no longer want things now, we want them yesterday! Yet in this high-speed world, we are called to be people of patience.

If the character quality of patience is going to grow in our lives, it is going to take effort on our parts. We need to recognize the danger and damage of impatience and commit ourselves to developing patience. The key to growing this characteristic in our lives is understanding the depth of God's patience toward us. When we realize His patience in the past and His continued patience toward us every day, we begin to tap into the source of patience that can fill and change our lives.

This session on patience is similar to the session on patience in the *Fruit of the Spirit* guide in the Interactions series. They were both drawn from the same resource material. Although the Snapshots are the same, the questions are different and move group members in a different direction. If your group has used the Interactions study *Fruit of the Spirit* recently, you may want to make a note of this, but point out that the questions will move the discussion in a whole new direction.

THE BIG PICTURE

Take time to read this introduction with the group. There are suggestions for how this can be done in the beginning of the leader's section.

A WIDE ANGLE VIEW

Question One Even the most patient people have moments when they wish they could take a patience pill. Take time for group members to honestly tell their stories of times when they experience the tension of impatience.

A BIBLICAL PORTRAIT

Read Luke 15:11–24

Questions Two & Three There were many ways the father in this story could have responded to his wayward son. He could have rejected him and slammed the door in his face. He could have punished him for his irresponsibility. He could have put the son on probation and given him a chance to earn back his father's trust. Or he could have done the very thing the son suggested—let him come back as a hired servant. But instead, he showed patience and love beyond description. This is because the father represents our God who is patient with His children, even when they don't realize it.

SHARPENING THE FOCUS

Read Snapshot "When Patience Runs Out, Watch Out!" before Question 4

Question Four Deep down we all know about the high price of impatience. I've often put it this way: "*When the patience runs out, watch out!*" That's when so much relational and professional damage is done. How many irresponsible marketplace decisions have been made in the heat of anger? How much spiritual damage is done when patience runs out?

When I was a kid in Michigan, exploding fireworks was illegal. But sometimes my dad's truck drivers would bring them up from another state. We would light a bunch of firecrackers and almost all of them would go off. However, there were always a few that did not explode. Their fuses had been burned down to only about 1/16" long, but they were still live. We all knew that if we lit a match, the second the match touched the fuse, it would explode immediately. We never wanted to play around with firecrackers with short fuses because we were afraid of getting our fingers blown off.

Relationships can be like this. If we are not careful, we can be deeply hurt by people with short fuses. Also, if we are honest, we must admit that we can hurt others when we have a short fuse and let anger get the best of us. Take time to tell your stories of the pain that has come from short fuses ignited by anger. When you pray together, be sure to lift up the broken hearts of those who have told about the damage they sustained because of relational or professional explosions they have experienced.

Read Snapshot "God's Patience with Unbelievers" before Question 5

Question Five I pray that the Holy Spirit will overwhelm every member of your small group with the amazing reality of God's patience toward them before they became Christians. I long for the day when people will say, "How did a Holy God put up with a sinner like me all of those years? How did He put up with my thoughts, values, goals, and morality? How did He put up with the fact that I was created to worship Him, and that I refused to?" When that realization hits us, we need to all cry out, "What a patient God! What a long-suffering God! What a forbearing God!"

With that realization, the Holy Spirit helps us see the length of God's fuse toward us. He then lengthens our fuse and fills us with His supernatural patience. Slowly, quietly, deeply, genuinely He changes our whole attitude toward other people. And because we realize God has been completely patient with us, we begin wanting to be patient with other people.

Read Snapshot "God's Patience with Believers" before Question 6

Questions Six & Seven I became a Christian when I was sixteen years old, and since then, I've broken all of the Ten Commandments, either mentally or actually. My guess is that you have also. I've said immature things in front of thousands of people. I've made unwise decisions, broken a series of promises, been both slothful and overzealous, both hateful and partial to others. Over time, the Holy Spirit has shown me who I really am. As I have seen His patience towards me, I've broken down and just said, "How patient our Lord has been to put up with me all these years."

Have you been a model Christian? Are you the picture of consistency? Are you a pillar of purity, faithfulness, loyalty, and single-mindedness? Have you loved the Lord your God with all your heart, soul, mind, and strength from the moment you received Christ? The truth is that we have all tested God's patience again and again. Still, He has proved patient even in the midst of our rebellion. What amazing patience! What an example for us to follow.

As we think about God's patience, the Holy Spirit says, "Take the hint. Lighten up with others. Loosen up. Give other people the same slack that God has given you. Show a little patience and grace." God has been exceedingly patient with you. Pass it on in your relationships with others.

Putting Yourself in the Picture

Challenge group members to take time in the coming week to use part or all of this application section as an opportunity for continued growth.

ENDURANCE
JAMES 1:2—4, 12

INTRODUCTION

In our high-speed world we demand overnight stardom, overnight success, overnight growth, overnight solutions, overnight spiritual maturity, and overnight marital bliss. If our expectations aren't met instantaneously and easily, there's a strong tendency in this culture to quit. So we quit jobs prematurely, drop out of educational programs, bail out of relationships, give up on our spiritual quests, and sometimes even give up on God's calling and mission for our lives. We don't understand this thing called "endurance."

God says we need endurance to face our daily challenges. Endurance is what sustains courage. Endurance gives staying power to discipline. Endurance sees to it that our visions become reality. You can do all the dreaming you want, but without endurance they become pipe dreams. You can't buy endurance and you can't bargain for it. But when you develop it over time, you will learn to see its value.

THE BIG PICTURE

Take time to read this introduction with the group. There are suggestions for how this can be done in the beginning of the leader's section.

A WIDE ANGLE VIEW

Question One All of us have stories of times we have quit or given up on someone or something. Some of these stories are light and humorous; others are deep and potentially painful. The stories can range from quitting tap dancing lessons in third grade to quitting on a marriage partner. Allow group members to tell their stories and pray for a trusting atmosphere as you begin to unearth some honest personal history.

A BIBLICAL PORTRAIT

Read James 1:2–4, 12

Question Two This passage says we ought to come to a point where we thank God for adversity because our adversities will enable us to develop endurance. When we face difficult times and endure through them, we grow stronger and more mature. The opposite is also true. If we lack endurance and tend to quit every time the pressure is on, we will find ourselves lacking maturity in many other areas of life. Endurance gives birth to deeper levels of endurance, while quitting tends to lead to more quitting.

Question Three Can we really find joy in the middle of suffering and struggle? The answer is yes! Invite group members to tell their own stories of deep joy in the midst of hard times. These testimonies to God's strength and faithfulness will be an encouragement for facing future struggles with endurance and faith.

SHARPENING THE FOCUS

Read Snapshot "Identifying Quitting Points" before Question 4

Questions Four & Five There are quitting points in every moral struggle. A quitting point is when you've been trying to be a godly man or woman, and you come to the point when you say, "It's not worth it anymore. Nobody else is struggling with this stuff. I think I'll cave in to the prevailing morals of the day." These are the moments you need to draw on endurance and stand strong.

There are also spiritual quitting points. A spiritual quitting point can occur when God is at work in your life. He's leading you down a path, but you're struggling and fighting and don't know if you can trust God. He says, "Come further. Just trust Me and follow Me." You get to the point where you say, "I'm the only one who is following God down this road and it seems like a dead end. I'm not going a step further. You promised that it's safe, but I don't think I can take another step!" That's a quitting point.

Sadly, Hollywood glamorizes quitting points. You've seen them so many times that you probably have never really thought about it consciously. There's a quitting point in the scene where a husband and wife are disagreeing. The tension is building. There does not seem to be much love left in the relationship. Finally, near the height of the frustration, as the music builds and the camera zooms in on their faces, the wife slaps her husband across the face, spins on her heels, and storms out of the house, slamming the door behind her. At this moment half the wives in America say, "That's what I want to do."

Too often we glamorize quitting. We forget that this couple is now heading for divorce court. Their children will suffer as they watch their parents go through the trauma of divorce. No one is going to win in this situation. But Hollywood makes millions with this lie.

Read Snapshot "Crashing Through Quitting Points" before Question 6

Questions Six & Seven There are many people who are about ready to cash in on their marriage. There were times early on in my own marriage where that became a very inviting option. It wasn't Lynne's fault; it was my own. But God was outrageously gracious to me and gave me the endurance I needed to hang in there. Other people kept saying, "Don't cash it in. Work it out. Fight for your marriage!" Over time God has changed my heart and helped me grow in many ways. I can honestly say that I would never trade in what Lynne and I have together. But it took endurance to push through those quitting points and make it to the place we are now.

Some believers have walked with God for many years and are tired of struggling. They are weary of the responsibility of living as a fully devoted follower of Christ. They say, "I'm just going to slip back to autopilot and become a spectator instead of a leader, a participant instead of a real servant." This is not what God wants us to do with our lives. We need to endure and keep living for God. We have to crash through these quitting points in order to see the joys that are on the other side!

Read Snapshot "Developing Endurance" before Question 8

Question Eight Close your group with some honest discussion about the areas in which you need to grow in endurance. Commit to pray for each other, support each other, and keep each other accountable in the coming months.

PUTTING YOURSELF IN THE PICTURE

Challenge group members to take time in the coming week to use part or all of this application section as an opportunity for continued growth.

CONTENTMENT

PSALM 103:1—13

INTRODUCTION

We live in a culture that believes in the myth of more. We are driven to gain more money, power, awards, fame, success, and many other things in the pursuit of happiness. We feel the void in our soul will stop aching if we can fill it with enough of these things. The problem is, these things don't satisfy. None of them can fill the void. Only when we have our hearts and lives filled with the love of God can we experience true contentment. You see, when we have Christ, we have everything—no matter what our bankbook or the most recent popularity polls say. And if we don't have Christ as our Savior, we have nothing . . . even if the world calls us rich. True contentment is not about what we have or accomplish. It is about who has us and what He has accomplished for us.

THE BIG PICTURE

Take time to read this introduction with the group. There are suggestions for how this can be done in the beginning of the leader's section.

A WIDE ANGLE VIEW

Question One We have all met people who are driven to have more, more, more! We might even see this kind of person when we look in the mirror every morning. Take time for honest reflection on the consequences of living a life driven by the desire for more.

A BIBLICAL PORTRAIT

Read Psalm 103:1–13

Questions Two & Three In this psalm King David says, "He satisfies my soul." What value can you place on having a satisfied soul? I wonder how many people we know could confidently say, "I have a satisfied soul. My cup is overflowing." According to this psalm, God provides all we need and so much more. Take time to read Psalm 103 and seek to get a clear picture of God's provision and character. In light of His commitment to watch over us and provide for us, encourage your group to draw a contrast between God's character and the character of a person who lives with discontentment.

SHARPENING THE FOCUS

Read Snapshot "The Myth of More" before Question 4

Questions Four & Five The media often fuels discontentment. Advertisers invest millions of dollars to convince people that their lives are incomplete without a lavishly furnished home, an imported automobile, and money left over to see the world. Mere exposure to thousands of thirty-second ads over the course of a year continues to pour fuel on the fires of discontentedness. A primary objective in the advertising industry is to create a feeling of deprivation which motivates people to purchase their way back to wholeness.

Peer pressure is another source of a growing heart of discontentedness. It starts when we are young. We see the things our friends and neighbors have and say, "I must have the kinds of things my friends have. If I don't, I will feel deprived. I will feel out of it. I will be discontented." I wish that I could say that these peer pressures subside when we reach adulthood, but they don't. Many adults act like big children. We must have what our peers have or we feel deprived. This is a lifelong battle. The toys change and get more expensive, but all through life we are driven by a desire to keep up with our friends in the acquisition of things.

Another source of discontentment is the old-fashioned sin of covetousness. It's probably been a while since you've spent much time reflecting on the tenth commandment. It says, "You shall not covet." This means we are not supposed to hunger for and desire what belongs to others. While growing up I used to wonder how the coveting prohibition ever made it into the top ten. I could understand how murder made the list, but what was the big deal about coveting? Over the years, I have learned that the sin of coveting is more serious than it first appears. Coveting is not simply admiring a particular commodity; it is being obsessed with the need to acquire that commodity, whatever it takes. Coveting compromises your values. It squeezes relationships out of your life. It blows the value of something way out of proportion. It is a poison we must all acknowledge and fight against.

Read Snapshot "Emptiness of Soul" before Question 6

Question Six There is great joy in telling our stories of life before we knew Jesus. This is not a time to glorify the sins of the past; it is a chance to remember what we have been saved from. As a leader, be sure the discussion moves toward celebrating the joy of knowing what we have been delivered from.

Question Seven As you reflect on all God has done for you and from what He has delivered you, be sure to remember that there are still people who are trapped in the empty pursuit of wanting more. Take time as a group to talk about the people in your life who don't yet know God's love. Encourage group members to pray for these people in the coming weeks.

You may want to pause at this time or at the end of the group to pray for these people by name. Celebrate the reality that all of your needs are met in Christ and pray for those who are still seeking.

Read Snapshot "Fullness of Soul" before Question 8

Question Eight What creates a contented attitude in a man or woman? What can satisfy a human being who lives in a world inebriated with materialism? What can satisfy a human being to the point of saying, "I have enough!"

The bottom line is knowing Christ personally. When you fellowship with Him regularly throughout the day, you discover what makes Christianity so unique. The essence of Christianity is a friendship, a relationship with God. The fullness of that relationship can be experienced throughout your everyday life. As you grow in Christ, you will sense His actual presence with you wherever you go, whether you're in your car, at the office, on the job site, at home, or at school. You'll become aware of His presence and you'll find yourself conversing with Him right in the middle of your day. It is this ever-present friendship factor that brings a whole new quality to life. Contentment is based on having your life filled with Jesus Christ. When you have Him, you have everything.

PUTTING YOURSELF IN THE PICTURE

Challenge group members to take time in the coming week to use part or all of this application section as an opportunity for continued growth.

ADDITIONAL WILLOW CREEK RESOURCES

Small Group Resources

Coaching Life-Changing Small Group Leaders, by Bill Donahue and Greg Bowman
The Complete Book of Questions, by Garry Poole
The Connecting Church, by Randy Frazee
Leading Life-Changing Small Groups, by Bill Donahue and the Willow Creek Team
The Seven Deadly Sins of Small Group Ministry, by Bill Donahue and Russ Robinson
Walking the Small Group Tightrope, by Bill Donahue and Russ Robinson

Evangelism Resources

Becoming a Contagious Christian (book), by Bill Hybels and Mark Mittelberg
The Case for a Creator, by Lee Strobel
The Case for Christ, by Lee Strobel
The Case for Faith, by Lee Strobel
Seeker Small Groups, by Garry Poole
The Three Habits of Highly Contagious Christians, by Garry Poole

Spiritual Gifts and Ministry

Network Revised (training course), by Bruce Bugbee and Don Cousins
The Volunteer Revolution, by Bill Hybels
What You Do Best in the Body of Christ—Revised, by Bruce Bugbee

Marriage and Parenting

Fit to Be Tied, by Bill and Lynne Hybels
Surviving a Spiritual Mismatch in Marriage, by Lee and Leslie Strobel

Ministry Resources

An Hour on Sunday, by Nancy Beach
Building a Church of Small Groups, by Bill Donahue and Russ Robinson
The Heart of the Artist, by Rory Noland
Making Your Children's Ministry the Best Hour of Every Kid's Week, by Sue Miller and David Staal
Thriving as an Artist in the Church, by Rory Noland

Curriculum

An Ordinary Day with Jesus, by John Ortberg and Ruth Haley Barton
Becoming a Contagious Christian (kit), by Mark Mittelberg, Lee Strobel, and Bill Hybels
Good Sense Budget Course, by Dick Towner, John Tofilon, and the Willow Creek Team
If You Want to Walk on Water, You've Got to Get Out of the Boat, by John Ortberg with Stephen and Amanda Sorenson
The Life You've Always Wanted, by John Ortberg with Stephen and Amanda Sorenson
The Old Testament Challenge, by John Ortberg with Kevin and Sherry Harney, Mindy Caliguire, and Judson Poling

Willow Creek Association
Vision, Training, Resources for Prevailing Churches

This resource was created to serve you and to help you build a local church that prevails. It is just one of many ministry tools that are part of the Willow Creek Resources® line, published by the Willow Creek Association together with Zondervan.

The Willow Creek Association (WCA) was created in 1992 to serve a rapidly growing number of churches from across the denominational spectrum that are committed to helping unchurched people become fully devoted followers of Christ. Membership in the WCA now numbers over 10,500 Member Churches worldwide from more than ninety denominations.

The Willow Creek Association links like-minded Christian leaders with each other and with strategic vision, training, and resources in order to help them build prevailing churches designed to reach their redemptive potential. Here are some of the ways the WCA does that.

- **A2: Building Prevailing Acts 2 Churches—Today**—an annual two-and-a-half day event, held at Willow Creek Community Church in South Barrington, Illinois, to explore strategies for building churches that reach out to seekers and build believers, and to discover new innovations and breakthroughs from Acts 2 churches around the country.

- **The Leadership Summit**—a once a year, two-and-a-half-day conference to envision and equip Christians with leadership gifts and responsibilities. Presented live at Willow Creek as well as via satellite broadcast to over one hundred locations across North America, this event is designed to increase the leadership effectiveness of pastors, ministry staff, volunteer church leaders, and Christians in the marketplace.

- **Ministry-Specific Conferences**—throughout each year the WCA hosts a variety of conferences and training events—both at Willow Creek's main campus and offsite, across the U.S., and around the world—targeting church leaders and volunteers in ministry-specific areas such as: evangelism, small groups, preaching and teaching, the arts, children, students, women, volunteers, stewardship, raising up resources, etc.

- **Willow Creek Resources®**—provides churches with trusted and field-tested ministry resources in such areas as leadership, evangelism, spiritual formation, spiritual gifts, small groups, stewardship, student ministry, children's ministry, the use of the arts-drama, media, contemporary music—and more.

- **WCA Member Benefits**—includes substantial discounts to WCA training events, a 20 percent discount on all Willow Creek Resources®, *Defining Moments* monthly audio journal for leaders, quarterly *Willow* magazine, access to a Members-Only section on WillowNet, monthly communications, and more. Member Churches also receive special discounts and premier services through WCA's growing number of ministry partners—Select Service Providers —and save an average of $500 annually depending on the level of engagement.

For specific information about WCA conferences, resources, membership, and other ministry services contact:

Willow Creek Association
P.O. Box 3188, Barrington, IL 60011-3188
Phone: 847-570-9812, Fax: 847-765-5046
www.willowcreek.com